People Say Hello

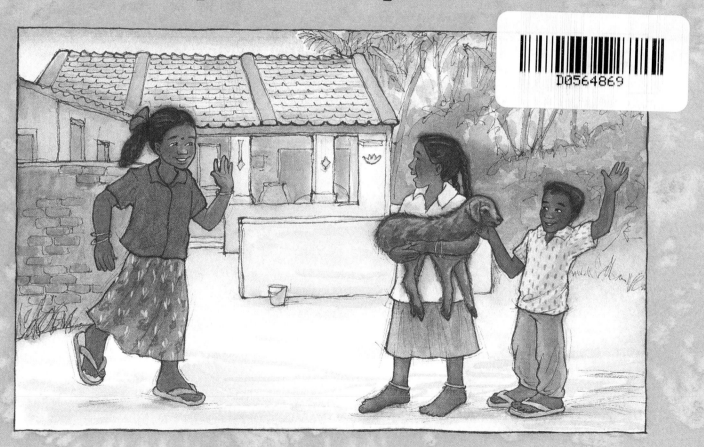

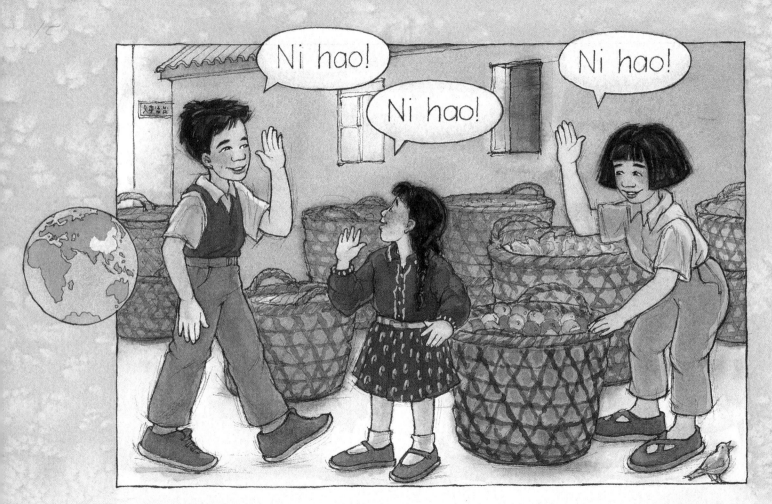

People say hello in China.

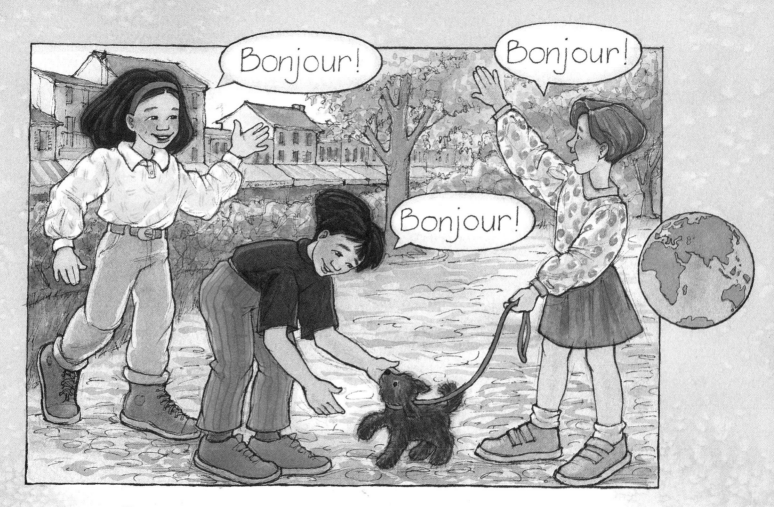

People say hello in France.

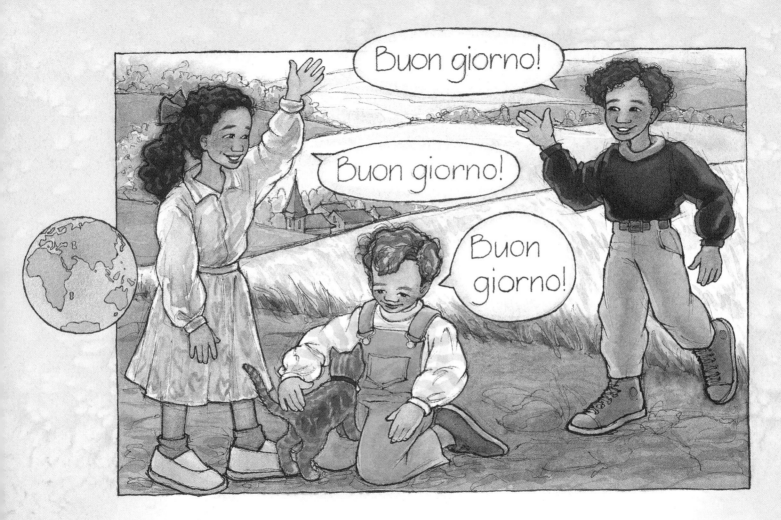

People say hello in Italy.

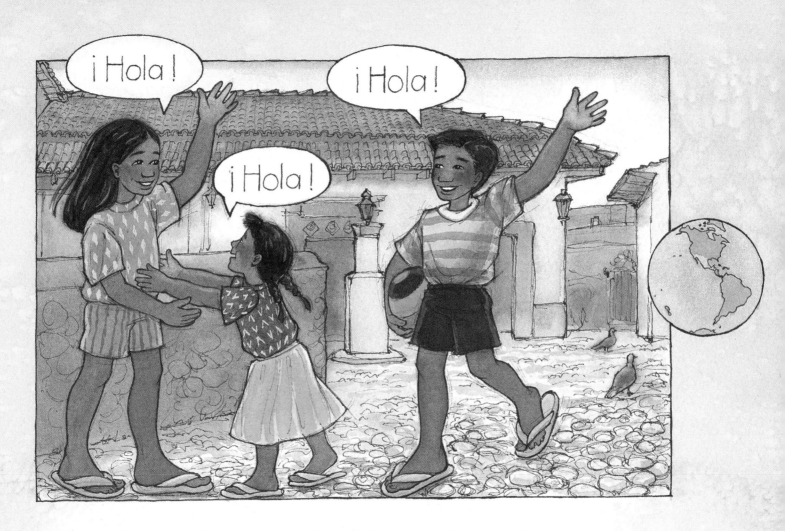

People say hello in Mexico.

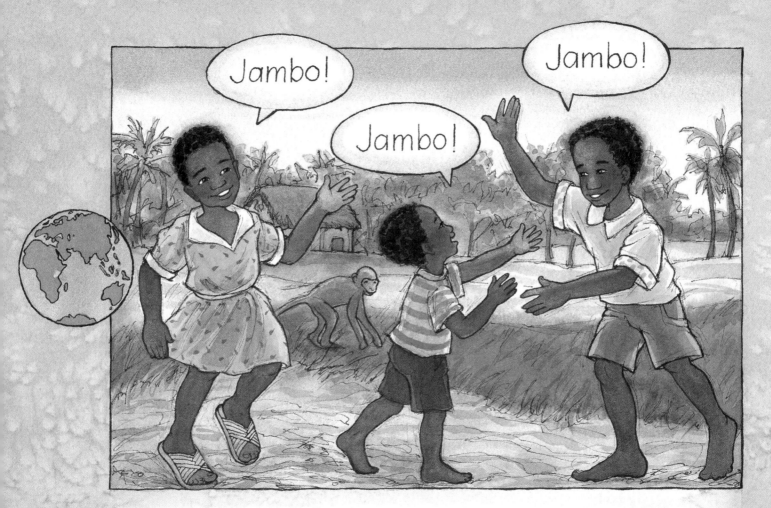

People say hello in Kenya.

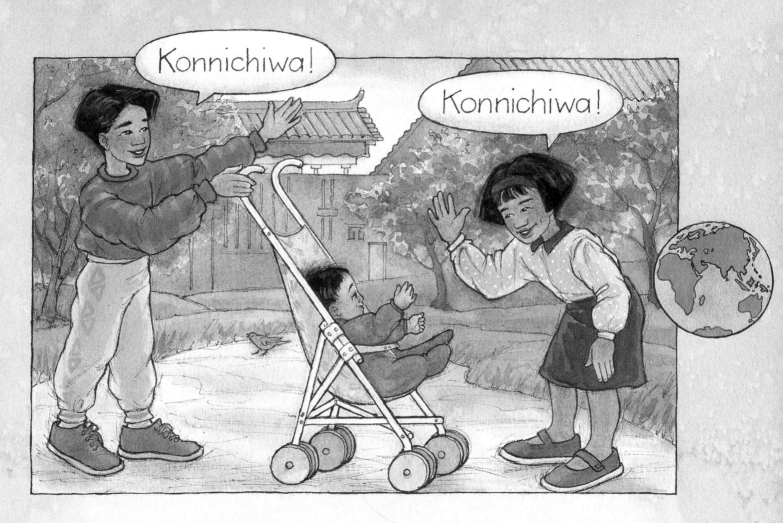

People say hello in Japan.

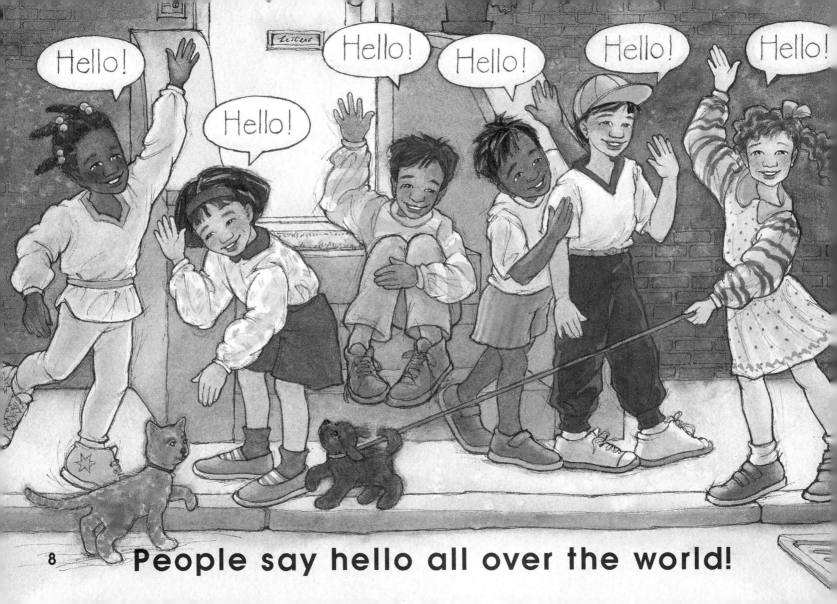

People say hello all over the world!